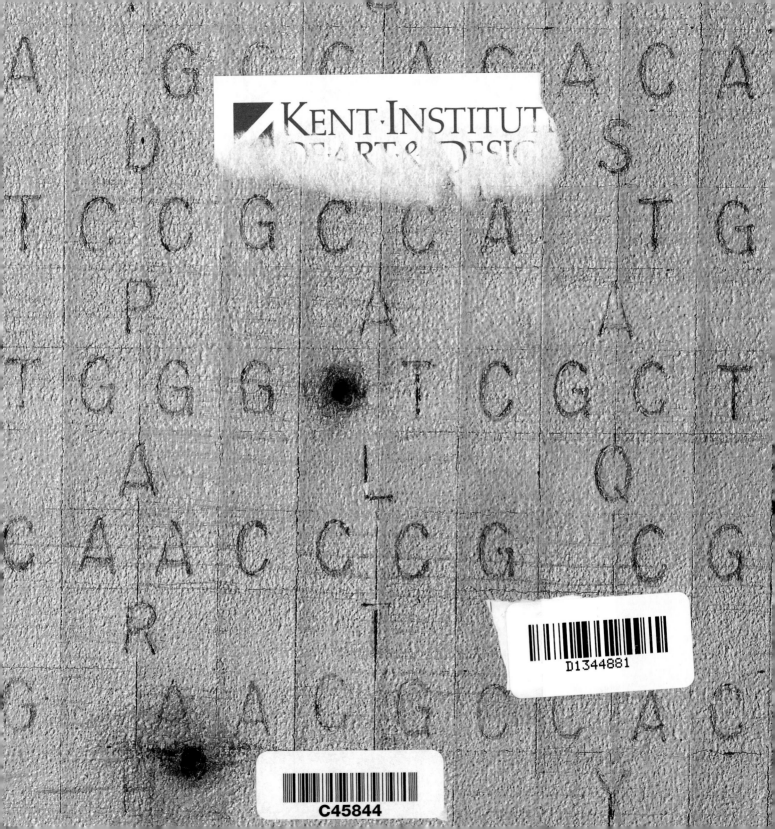

Author: Helga Pakasaar
Series Editor & Graphic Design:
Matthew Koumis
Printed in England by
Offset Colour Print, Southampton

© **Telos Art Publishing 2002**
PO Box 125, Winchester
SO23 7UJ England
T   +44 (0) 1962 864546
F   +44 (0) 1962 864727
E   editorial@telos.net
E   sales@telos.net
W   www.arttextiles.com

ISBN 1 902015 35 5 (softback)
ISBN 1 902015 52 5 (hardback)

A CIP catalogue record for this book is
available from The British Library

Note
All dimensions are shown in imperial and
metric, height x width x depth.

Photo Credits
Tim Thayer, E.G. Schempf, Casey Sills,
Michael Spillers, Daniel O'Connor

Artist's Acknowledgements
Much appreciation is extended to Irene
Hofmann, Buzz Spector, and Helga
Pakasaar for their thoughtful writings and
to Susan Snodgrass for editorial advice.

I would like graciously to thank Sarah
Wagner, Lori Tampa, Rebecca Kinnee and
Lynn Bennett-Carpenter for assistance in
the studio. I am grateful to John Rowland
Workshop, Richmond Stampworks and to
Mike Paradise.

My projects are always enhanced by the
enduring advice and support of Thomas
Lehn.

Thanks to Cranbrook Academy of Art for
a grant in partial support of this
monograph.

Cover Illustrations:
front:
stanza (detail) 2001
dictionary, gesso, wax, laser engraving,
polyurethane
9.75 x 7.75 x 1.5in

back:
SNPS/slips 4 (detail) 2002
dictionary, laser engraving,
lacquer/wood frame
20 x 24 x 2.75in
(50 x 60 x 6.88cm)

illustration on page 1:
column 1 (detail) 1997
acrylic on cork, masonite
24 x 12 x 1in
(60 x 30 x 2.5cm)

portfolio collection
Jane Lackey

TELOS

Contents

6   **Biography**

11   **Foreword**
      by Irene Hofmann

14   **Distillations**
      by Helga Pakasaar

40   **Colour Plates**

archive
Installation, Cranbrook Art Museum
1999
left to right: **hive, blot, diaries**

Biography

| **Born** | 1948, Chattanooga, Tennessee |

Education and Awards

1974	BFA, California College of Arts and Crafts, Oakland, California
1979	MFA, Cranbrook Academy of Art, Bloomfield Hills, Michigan
1984,88	National Endowment for the Arts, Individual Artist Fellowship
1989	United States/France Visual Artist Residency, La Napoule, France
1996-95	Margaret Hall Silva Foundation Grant, Grand Arts, Kansas City, Missouri
1997	Illinois Arts Council Artists Fellowship Award

Selected Solo Exhibitions

2002	'Jane Lackey,' Roy Boyd Gallery, Chicago, Illinois
2000	'Jane Lackey,' Dolphin, Kansas City, Missouri
	'Jane Lackey, Joan Livingstone,' Roy Boyd Gallery, Chicago, Illinois
1999	'archive, an installation of new work by Jane Lackey,' Cranbrook Art Museum
1998	'Jane Lackey,' Sybaris Gallery, Royal Oak, Michigan
1997	'tabulations,' Roy Boyd Gallery, Chicago, Illinois
1996	'in code,' Grand Arts, Kansas City, Missouri
1995	'Jane Lackey,' Sybaris Gallery, Royal Oak, Michigan
1994	'Jane Lackey: Recent Works,' I Space, Chicago, Illinois
	'Recent Works: Jane Lackey & Warren Seelig,' Gallery of Art, Johnson County Community College, Overland Park, Kansas
1993	'Jane Lackey - A Decade of Work,' Textile Art Center, Chicago, Illinois
1988	'Jane Lackey,' Hokin/Kaufman Gallery, Chicago, Illinois
1982	'Jane Lackey,' Charlotte Crosby Kemper Gallery, Kansas City Art Institute, Kansas City, Missouri

Selected Group Exhibitions

2002	'The Bones of Clouds: Some Recent Experiences of Chance,' Center Galleries, Detroit, Michigan
	'Side by Side,' Dolphin, Kansas City, Missouri
	Roy Boyd Gallery, Chicago, Illinois
2001	'On Language: Text and Beyond,' Center Galleries, Detroit, Michigan
	'(Embrace) Midwesterness,' Arena Gallery, Chicago Illinois
2000	'Paradise Now, Picturing the Genetic Revolution', Exit Art, New York (tour/Tang Museum)
	'Remnants of Memory,' Asheville Art Museum, Asheville, N Carolina
	'Critical Eyes', MoNA - The Museum of New Art, Pontiac, Michigan
	'Fast: Five Years at Grand Arts,' Grand Arts, Kansas City, Missouri
1999	'Cranbrook: Postopia,' City of Los Angeles Craft and Folk Art Museum,
1998	'Trans,' Gallery NC, Pusan, South Korea
1997	'Off the Map,' Paint Creek Center for the Arts, Rochester, Michigan
1996	'Cloth Reveries,' Janet Wallace Fine Arts Center, Saint Paul, Minnesota
1993	'Pushing the Boundaries,' Evanston Art Center, Evanston, Illinois
	'Domestic Ontogeny: New Textile Forms,' Oliver Art Center, Oakland, California
	'Nine Women,' Dart Gallery, Chicago, Illinois
1992	'New American Talent,' Laguna Gloria Art Museum, Austin, Texas
1991	'Perspectives from the Pacific Rim,' Bellevue Art Museum, Bellevue, Washington
1989	'14th International Biennial of Tapestry,' Musee Cantonal des Beaux-Arts, Lausanne
1986	'Poetry of the Physical,' American Craft Museum, New York (Tour Europe)

Works in Public Collections

Detroit Institute of the Arts, Detroit, Michigan
Michener Collection, Gallery of Art, Kent State University, Kent, Ohio
Nelson Atkin Museum of Art, Print Collection, Kansas City, Missouri
Hallmark Fine Art Collection, Kansas City, Missouri
American Craft Museum, New York
Stowers Institute for Medical Research, Kansas City, Missouri
Informax, Inc., Bethesda, Maryland
The Sigal Corporation, Washington, D.C.
TIAA-CREF Fine Art Collection, St. Louis, Missouri
Johnson County Community College, Permanent Collection, Overland Park, Kansas
Xerox Corporation, Washington, D.C.

Commissions

Stowers Institute for Medical Research

Selected Publications and Reviews

2002	*Art Tomorrow,* Edward Lucie-Smith, Vilo International, Paris, France
	Paradise Now: Picturing the Genetic Revolution, edited by Ian Berry
	(exhibition catalogue) Tang Museum, DAP, New York
2001	'Waiting, She Missed Nothing,' Gerry Craig, Winter, *Surface Design Journal*
2000	*DNART,* review by Peter Schjeldahl, *The New Yorker,* Oct.2
	'Our Language, Our Selves,' review by Kate Hackman, *Kansas City Star,* Sep 22
	Art Textiles of the World: USA, edited by Matthew Koumis,
	Telos Art Publishing, Winchester, GB
	New Art Examiner, March, review by Jenni Sorkin
	American Craft, Spring, review by Polly Ullrich
	Opening Position Opening Form, essay by Tim Porges, Roy Boyd Gallery

1999	'arc*hive,' an installation of new works by Jane Lackey*, exhibition essay by Irene Hofmann, Cranbrook Art Museum, Bloomfield Hills, Michigan
1997	NO: Nouvel Object, Artists Portfolio, Design House, Seoul, Korea
1997	'Lost in a Sea of Shapes,' *Chicago Reader*, Sept 19, review by Fred Camper
	'A Phenomenology of Dirt', article by William Easton, *Surface Design Journal*, Spring
1996	in code, exhibition essay by A. Laurie Palmer, Grand Arts, Kansas City, Missouri
1994	*Art News*, November, review by Garrett Holg
1993	*Artistes à La Napoule*, La Napoule Art Foundation, Isabelle Maheu-Viennot, Éditions du Cygne, France

Professional

Artist-in-Residence, Cranbrook Academy of Art, Bloomfield Hills, Michigan
Represented by Roy Boyd Gallery, Chicago, Illinois ; Dolphin, Kansas City, Missouri

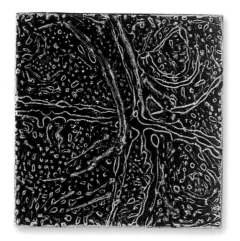

above:
aerolae 2
1995
collagraph, ink on paper
5 x 5in (12 x 12cm)

page 12:
column 4
1999
acrylic, ink on cork, masonite
84 x 12 x 0.5in (210 x 30 x 12cm)

Foreword

Jane Lackey creates works that explore the territory between art, science and linguistics, recalling the highly organized systems inherent in such ordered structures as the human genome or a dictionary of the English language. From these complex sources and sets of information, Lackey finds analogies to abstraction and textile production as she synthesizes their individual modes of notation and organization into poetic forms, patterns and methods of mark making. Her works engage vast archives of data, both visible and invisible, ordered and random, reliable and flawed, revealing richly-layered metaphors for understanding human identity and knowledge.

In early works, the interior operations and hidden codes of the human body become the source of patterns and gestures that suggest the intricacy of the body's interior data and the invisible markers of individual characteristics.

"Fingerprints", "blots" and "smears" become both formal strategies for Lackey's exquisite marks and linguistic indicators of the complex biological source of her patterns. Most recently, language structures have come to the forefront in works titled *'SNPS/slips'*, as manipulated dictionary pages and their worn cloth-bound covers become the site for explorations of slippages and mis-orderings in language and science.

Considering a decade of Lackey's works reveals a rigorous exploration of the invisible traits and codes of the human body and how such ordered systems can inform a stunning visual vocabulary of evocative patterns, surfaces and forms.

Irene Hofmann

Curator of Contemporary Art
Orange County Museum of Art,
Newport Beach

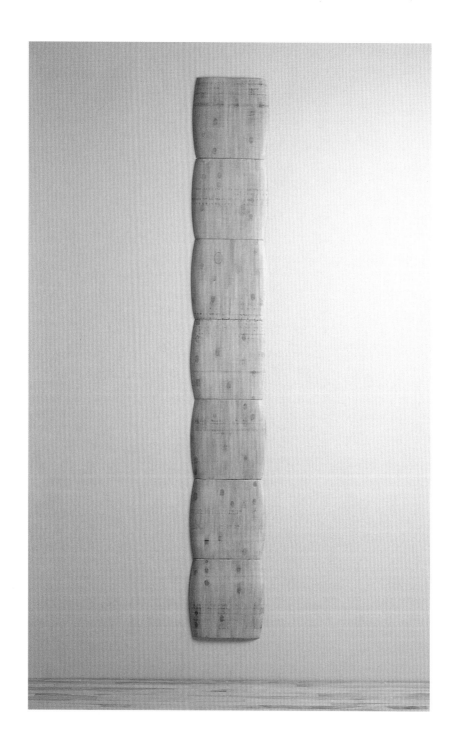

Distillations

by Helga Pakasaar

Distillations

Self-contained, delicately nuanced, intimate and serene. It is these qualities of Jane Lackey's artworks that are their gentle lure, and that inspire an equally attentive response. The artist manages to return the language of technology, with all its cold bits, bites, and codes, to an imaginary space that is intimately tied to the materiality of the human body. This process of retrieval and translation is a type of dance that recasts the complex profusion of visual stimuli and information into a material dream space. In this sense, Lackey transcribes the collective hallucination of technology into private reverie. Imagine the scene in the film 'Dancer in the Dark' when a blind factory worker begins tapping out the rhythms of noisy machinery, gradually falling in sync into an ecstatic dance. Her empowered voice soars in concert with the mechanical din, then the spell breaks. Similarly, Lackey's artworks are assertions of modest human expression that talk back to the gargantua of technology through body language.

As if in a trance herself, the artist methodically enacts laborious procedures. Her controlled repetitive gestures come from precise, calibrated movements that imitate the mechanistic. The intricacies of this dialogue with technological language is manifest in the sheer density of the abstract fields of Lackey's artworks.

How individuals change in relation to technological culture is the underlying question that Lackey's artwork posits. Neither ironic nor desperately seeking to decode the ineffable — like so many artists grappling with this subject — she adapts the methodical logic and sign systems of technology to reinscribe that knowledge with human physicality. Her artworks reveal the traces of this encounter in which she negotiates, domesticates, plays, and argues with languages of representation, especially those of science. The languages are distilled into intricate patterns of lines, blips, numbers, letters, and incisions of various kinds.

Intrigued by how vast amounts of information reduced to signs and coding systems still carry profound human meanings, she articulates the intersections of knowledge and perception by weaving the senses into rationalized spaces. For this artist, the desire to leave marks makes no claims for subjectivity or an authentic self. Instead, she provides tangible expression of the need to index and organize in order to understand the world. This process of cognitive mapping is a way to analyse and reduce the chaos of existing things to some kind of order. In navigating through the interstitial spaces of the decipherable and the invisible, the artist interweaves conceptual and sensory experience.

Lackey has maintained a preoccupation with translating the immaterial into the material realm since the late 1970s.

Always concerned with the social histories associated with textiles, she became inspired by Arte Povera's evocative use of subtle gesture and mundane materials, as well as by a range of artists expanding the field of painting through alternative materials and processes, such as Lucio Fontana and Eva Hesse. The early work focused on textile constructions and works on paper. In a series of large black woven pieces from the early 1980s, she explored appearing and disappearing marks through the process of dyeing and bleaching individual threads. These black fields punctuated by lines dissolving into specks of colour were reminiscent of the spatial ambiguities of night skies. She then developed a series of sculpted weavings that involved hooking brightly coloured telephone wires into the warp of cloth, creating a pile that projected a haze of colour out from the surface.

The stiff but flexible properties of the wire that activated the physical surface referred to drawing. In all of Lackey's works, the activity of drawing involves a mental and physical mapping that is driven by a nervous energy communicated through the body. This sense of the physical in dialogue with the intellect has become more pronounced in her works of the past decade that continue to increase in spatial and sculptural presence.

Lackey's art of twenty years offers a sustained meditation on the impact of social structures on human senses and consciousness. The deliberate and labour-intensive procedures of her art production allow this inquiry to play out on various levels. Still informed by a sensibility strongly tied to the medium of fiber, Lackey has maintained a commitment to a material-based practice that embraces aspects of photography, painting, sculpture, and digital media.

She continues to expand her inventory of materials, and the vocabulary of textile construction through threading and unravelling, in both literal and metaphorical ways. The physical properties of woven cloth are reflected in abstract fields of pattern, fabricated from accretions of methodical gesture and mark making. She draws on diverse sources and historical references, and takes into account that weaving systems have influenced many advanced technologies such as microchips and computers.[1]
In keeping with the tactile, mutable allure of fabric, she favours industrial materials such as cork and felt that retain a certain plasticity as well as reveal their fabrication. Their forgiving surfaces are responsive to the artist's manipulations of staining, scoring, scraping, puncturing and imprinting. Once glued onto shaped masonite or bent plywood, these surfacing materials are coated with many thin layers of paint.

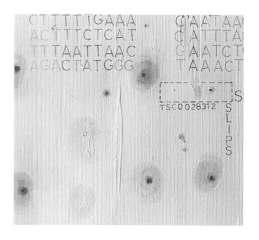

smear (3)
2000
acrylic, ink on cork, birch plywood
44.5 x 45 x 4in (111 x 112 x 10cm)
Informax, Inc., Maryland

Impeccably crafted and detailed, Lackey's material paintings are handmade productions. Never flat, their curvilinear and beveled forms often reveal intricately painted backsides and seem to resonate in space. Lackey's sculpted paintings initially read as atmospheric abstractions. Upon closer scrutiny, however, a cacophony of pattern and texture emerge from the worried surfaces. Thin glazes of white and grey mask layers of bright colour underneath that pop out with detonated vibrancy where the surface is punctured.

The artist's abiding concern with the rhetoric of abstraction grounds the works in a common language. Reductivism is also a means to evoke the *tabula rasa* of (mis)recognition that enables the ordering of space. What initially appears unreadable is only a latent blankness, a cipher waiting for the viewer's projection. Her paintings call for studied observation, compelling us to scan repeatedly their encrusted surfaces, to uncover and decipher layers of meaning.

This perceptual drift through accretions of inscripted data never resolves into a picture, but rather remains a dense field that perpetually mutates. This effect has more to do with the poetics of technology, than the discourses of modernist painting. Lackey's paintings defy traditional categories, such as landscape, figuration, and abstraction, by indirectly embracing all genres simultaneously. Evoking the immaterial glow of electronic screens, their apparent blankness is not inert but, rather, a condition of charged anticipation. Their torqued shapes allude to receptors that capture and transmit information – speakers, mirrors, sensors, computer screens, satellite dishes, tablets – and their layered webs of patterned data are akin to structures of advanced imaging systems. Subtle and restrained, these perceptual fields of grid and gesture have a quiet power similar to that of an Agnes Martin painting. As meditative expressions of the unrepresentable, they approach the contemporary sublime. [2]

Lackey's interest in scientific perceptions of living matter takes into account how analogue and digital imaging systems mediate knowledge and experience. For example, the work *'magnifications, cells 1 and 2'* (1993) suggests cellular activity as seen through a microscope or, perhaps, telescopic views of a night sky. These larger-than-life sized cells are incised with marks burnt into the felt ground. The *sfumato* effect of the fluid network of arteries and nuclei seem to move in and out of focus, as if throbbing with energy. Skirmishing between macro and micro associations, *'cell I and 2'* appear to be suspended in a state of mitosis, as do the cell-like forms that animate their surfaces. Whether enlargements of minutiae or miniaturized views of infinite spaces, these cells seem without any coordinates, adrift in an ambiguous time and space. These scapes are placed in direct relation to the observer's body, emphasizing their disorienting effect and further

confusing our perception and haptic understanding. They underscore how empirical evidence revealed by optical instruments creates a fragmentary sense of the real, and they amplify the alienation that comes from apprehending the body's interior.

The elegant ellipsis, *'mundi'* (1994) evokes a landscape, reiterated by the horizontal format. More worked and layered, its encrusted skin seems bruised and wrinkled with forceful burns in earth tones that seem to blossom sporelike growths. Barely legible fragments of phototransfers of the body's vascular system, xeroxed from medical books, are also imbedded in the ground. The intricate scapes of *'magnifications'* and *'mundi'* are mapped with scars produced by singeing the felt grounds with a burning tool, then they are coated with acrylic stains and sealed with a skin of translucent wax. Veiled under this screen suggestive of the clinical gaze of forensic science, the

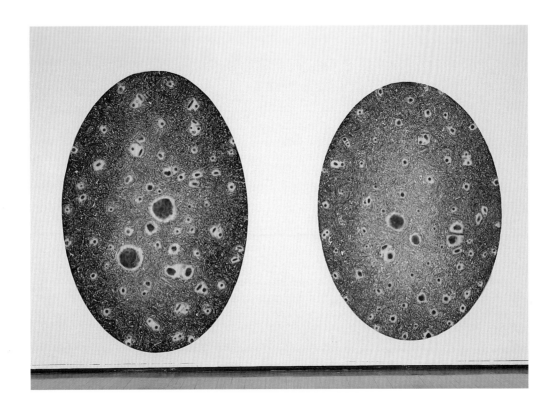

magnifications: cell 1 & 2

installation, Evanston Art Center, Illinois

1993

acrylic, oil ,wax, burned felt

(1) 88 x 66 x 5in (224 x 167 x 13cm) (right hand side)

(2) 95 x 65 x 5in (241 x 162 x 13cm) (left hand side)

19

mundi

1994

acrylic, oil, wax, photo transfers, burned felt

20 x 54 x 1in (51 x 137 x 2cm)

protective membrane on the giant tissue specimens does little to disguise the visceral interiors. Just as the artist is involved in an activity of excavation and retrieval, the viewer is inspired to forage through the fields of energy and matter in search of knowledge. The sensuality of these elusive works solicits an embodied encounter.

Lackey's artwork proposes that as medical technology probes ever deeper into the immaterial and invisible interior of the body, how the material processes of life actually work remains mysterious. 21st Century genetics now endeavours to map the human body through a universal language that conceives of human bodies as systems of programmed information. Lackey tests the efficacy of this explanation for human existence by asking how can sentient beings relate to such a proposal?

The impact of medical science on identity is explored in *'traits'* (1996), an installation of twelve clusters of small basswood forms that resemble medical images of gyrating chromosomes. Each of the 46 pieces began as the shape of a splitting cell, then was altered through sanding, shaping, cutting, and burning until it assumed an individual identity, and was finally catalogued in one of the twelve variations. Displayed as constellations encircling a room, the traits emerge from the wall as if a type of Braille or calligraphy. The message, however, is scrambled and indecipherable. Although science has given shape and form to invisible matter, scientific theories can be slippery. This piece implies that to distinguish between desirable and undesirable traits, and to define individuals by a generalized template, is highly problematic.

traits
installation (partial view)
Grand Arts, Kansas City, Missouri
1996
·spackle/acrylic on burned basswood
30 x 144 x 1in (75 x 360 x 2cm)

Ultimately, the complexity and social meaning of scientific theory cannot be translated into visual language.
It is this very discrepancy, the gap between perception and knowledge, that is of primary interest to the artist. As she has written: "Questions which involve predetermination, disease, mutation, equality, fate, transformation, transgression, morality, variation, fragility and extinction are seated in these phenomena which in appearance alone are fuzzy paired strands of fibrous material." [3]

In the painting series, *'marker'* (1996), Lackey explores further questions of individual identity in relation to medical templates. "These works refer to medical tests that register vital information by fluid staining and mirror a condition or a specific profile," says the artist. "In a very abstract way this kind of medical information can be thought of as a portrait." [4] In these tall elliptical shapes, surfaced with cork, identity is rendered as nothing more than random sequences of abstract pattern.

The monumental, somber "portraits" seem to hover in a luminous state of grace. Their pale grey/green skin is blotched with burn marks and sculpted by incisions, stains, and scars that secrete undercoatings of bright color. A mechanistic pattern of dots and dashes, rendered with pressure from a hot tip, scurry across the topographic surfaces like Morse code, a mechanical tapping out of a language activated by touch. Suggestive of video screens, their greyish fields, gridded and pixelated in candy colours, hum with a modulated frequency. Sometimes faint and sometimes loud, the visual chatter emanating from each work infiltrates systemic order with personal agency. As if the consequence of a machine, the precision of the artist's repetitive mark making accommodates chance encounters, mistakes and the contingent. The dynamic created by this weaving of technological language into a corporeal terrain intimates the tension between the brain and the senses. As the title implies, the marker appropriately edged in red refers to textile, genetic and computer terms as well as social locators.

marker 3 & 4
1996
acrylic on cork, masonite
each 77 x 34 x 1in (192 x 85 x 2cm)
Detroit Institute of the Arts (marker 3)

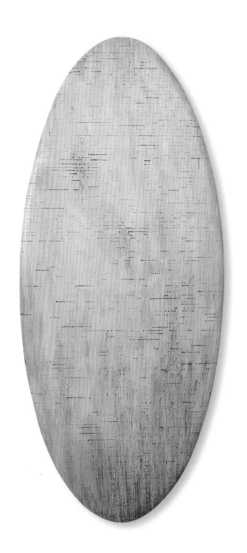

In *'columns'* (1997-) and *'receptors'* (2001), identity is represented as a code of letters and numbers culled from genetic mappings. In these works, Lackey strings together DNA sequence, pattern and imprint found in medical journals and other technical sources, allowing for the interpretative mistakes that inevitably result from transcription. Her coded messages of seemingly random patterns are counterpoints that indicate a persuasive form of human intelligence. Guided by intuition, revealed in the vibrant traces of her physical gestures of fingerprinting and staining, she insists that knowledge, based in the senses, is inchoate. In this way, she gives expression to the oldest meaning of the term gene: *becoming*.

Lackey understands that the social meanings of DNA cannot be reduced to a sequence of letters. Just as any text is animated by the reader's projection, so too, the realization of genetic code adapts to context. After all, it is how DNA bonds with the particular chemistry of an organism that is most relevant to determining identity. Her works support Michel Foucault's argument that "real language is not a totality of independent signs.

It is rather an opaque, mysterious thing, closed in upon itself, a fragmented mass, its enigma renewed in every interval, which combines here and there with the forms of the world and becomes interwoven with them." [5] Lackey's reflections on genetics imply that DNA is "the accomplice of truant bodies," [6] where chance and anomaly are significant. In *'columns'*, for example, DNA sequencing – represented by four nucleotide bases of A (adenine), T (thymine), C (cytosine), G (guanine) – covers the sensual columnar forms in a continuous feed of data. As the series progresses, rows of evenly spaced letters give way to uneven groupings and, finally, are clustered into 'sentences,' becoming a more personal language. Red editing circles that refer to reading, sorting, and decoding form another layer of random pattern. Like genetic code, the underlying grid in Lackey's works accommodates and potentially corrects aberrations, mistakes, and idiosyncrasies, yet still has a regulatory power. Implicit in the artist's act of 'fingerprinting' is the critical question of whether medical science will empower humanity or destroy our individuality.

column 1

1997

acrylic on cork, masonite

24 x 12 x 1in (60 x 30 x 2cm)

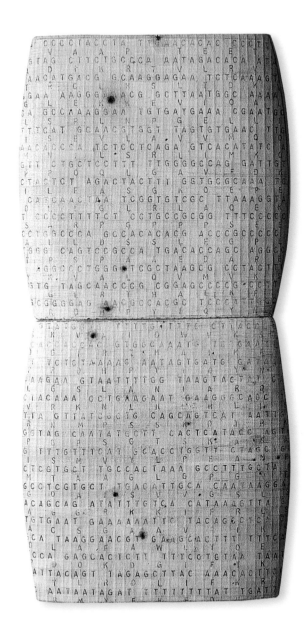

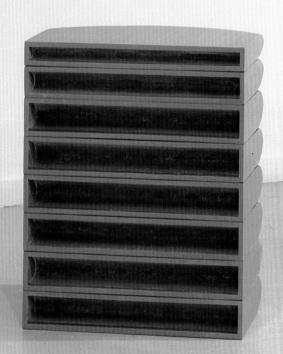
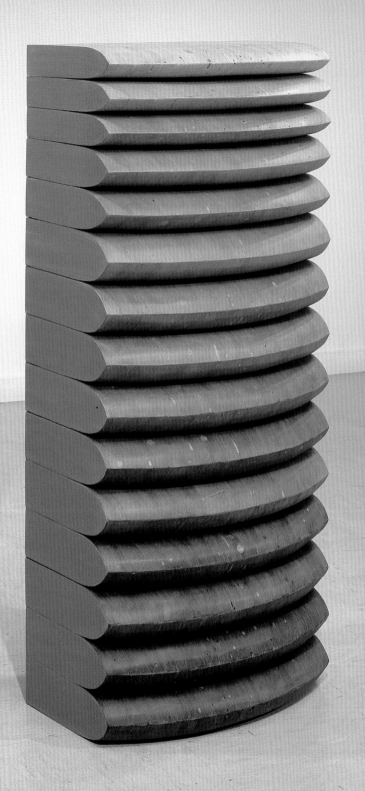

hive
1999
acrylic on cork, MDF board,
polyurethane
33 x 25 x 12in (82 x 62 x 30cm)
58 x 25 x 12in (145 x 62 x 30cm)

After all, the authority of such evidence has long been discredited as a disguised form of social control. Thus in these works, Lackey reckons with the broad social implications of the life sciences.

Especially in light of human genomics, Lackey's project proposes the necessity for a new pictorialism, a new aesthetic language for expressing our experiential understanding and sense of the body. The classic image of the human figure as an entity defined by its boundaries is, perhaps, no longer a sufficient way to picture lived experience. More than simply an insinuation of the material body on fields of immaterial data and artifice, Lackey's approach is based in a philosophical imperative to translate contemporary technologies of perception through the haptic. Over the past ten years, the artist's hand has become more physically direct, creating a sense of intimacy also reflected in the reduced scale of the works. Initially marks were made using a burning pencil and small scrapers, followed by more tactile Q-tip marks, then directly through fingerprinting.

In a new work in progress, entitled *'genePool'*, the spectator is enveloped in a spatial installation of large receptors punctuated by recorded sounds of voices. With this movement towards spatial immediacy and human presence as a form of encryption, Lackey's artworks have become increasingly schematic and abstract.

This movement towards an increasingly embodied interface could be interpreted as a response to the condition of information becoming more accessible, while at the same time, knowledge becomes more remote and impersonal. As global economies are increasingly interconnected with technological and collective systems, the singularity of the individual is destabilized. In this context, *'hive'* (1999) – a sculpture that alludes to the natural structure of the beehive – seems an appropriate metaphor. The sculpture is made of twenty-three curved wood forms covered in cork that, painted in greens and browns, is layered with marks, smears, fingerprints, and burn holes.

As an archive that results from collective swarming and pooling of information, the beehive represents the beauty of a natural coded language of mutuality. As one of the first animal language systems to be decoded, it has served as a model for advanced technologies.[7] The internet's vectors and accretions of data could also be thought of as a type of hive, an indeterminate communal space that results from chains of communication. The stacked, compressed form of *'hive'* refers to storage systems that as material objects reveal nothing of the immaterial information they contain. This work also recalls a library of stacked books, an archive of inaccessible and hidden information. Containers, frames, and archival systems are the defining elements that determine the limits, not the substance, of Lackey's works. The body as a bounded system is continually modified through changing social contexts and ideological constructs. Her works have increasingly taken on the character of palimpsests as the body is reduced to an abstract language, a composite of designs overwritten by other texts.

The *'receptor'* (2000) series of convex and concave disks articulates this matrix of body and language. In addition to referring to the nomenclature of laboratory procedures, titles such as *'blot'*, *'smear'*, and *'receptors:scrape/swab'* evoke a guttural, embodied language that also connotes various social stigmas. As in all of her works, the *'receptors'* are not meant to signify the real or index something else, but rather function as a synecdoche — the part representing the whole. Defying the promises of modern technology (to unify knowledge and experience within a single frame), these images make no claims for grasping totalities. Rather, they offer horizons of possibility where the general and the particular coexist. Always allowing for the risk of getting lost in the minutiae of detail, the artist gives full range to the poetics and significance of the particular. Her finicky attention to detail is a feminist strategy that entices us to drift through surface sensations, taking pleasure in the decorative and, perhaps, becoming seduced by excessive visual stimuli.[8]

"Limited to two marks – dots and dashes, the patterns mix codes that refer to sound and explore the physical motion of scraping and swabbing while following a disciplined binary system of mapping." [9]

receptors: scrape/swab (2)
2001
acrylic, ink on cork, birch plywood
each 33 x 32 x 5.5in (82 x 80 x 14cm)

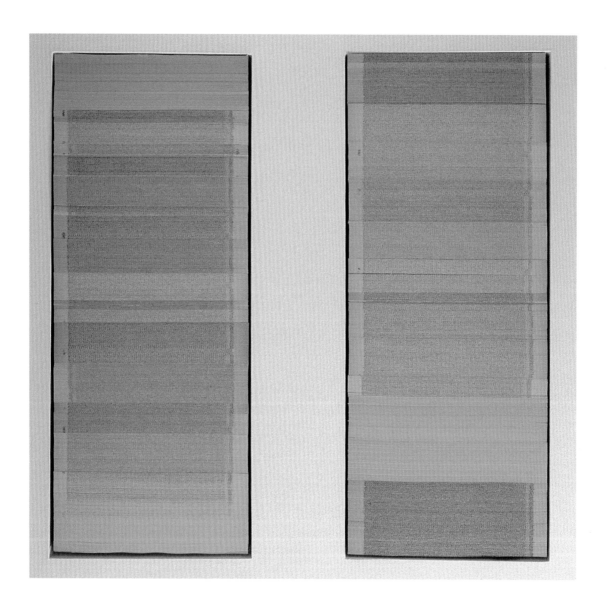

Lackey's most recent works incorporate another immense system of information – the dictionary. One could say that the comprehensive ambitions of dictionaries mimic those of science. As cultural artifacts of organized knowledge, they too are inherently tied to systems of naming and ordering. Like maps, dictionaries imply that what is not named does not exist. And like genetic code, its alphabetical logic is the internal sequence of letters. The presence of well-used thumb indexes – another sorting device – serve as reminders of our tactile relationship to language. As in earlier pieces, knowledge in these works is presented as an idea, but is locked away, rendered mute. In 'stanza' (2002), for example, word patterns are hidden under gesso, then replaced by letters of the genome (in a convergence of language systems) . The pages of the dictionaries have been sliced such that printed words

contained inside are silenced, and seen only as a fuzzy pattern of ink on the edges of the cut pages. In 'new centuries: vol. 1 and 2' (2000), the subtle patterning of lines resonate like a poor digital scan and reveals the act of slicing as a scanning process. The way that the pattern of lines dissolves into grey bits is similar to the visual effect of Ikat weaving. Although minimalist in gesture and appearance, this piece enlivens the tactile, visual, and aural senses.

new centuries: vol. 1 and 2
2000
dictionaries, polyurethane
each column:26 x 10.5 x 1.75in
(65 x 26 x 4cm)

Embodied speech is presented literally in *'SNPS/slips'* (2002) a series of twelve dictionaries in various languages and sizes. The dictionary pages have been sliced and paired with their hard covers, the storage containers of written language. Some covers offer clues to content – The Secretary's Deskbook, Iwananis Worterbuch Deutsch-Japanisch, embossed insignias – but most reveal only the vestiges of their pages. Obviously well used, they are displayed like specimens or historical artifacts. Into the ordered grid and logic of the display system, Lackey has inserted sequences of words and numbers on the covers, introducing other language systems. The reference numbers and letters of genetic sequences are called SNPS (locations where one person's genes differ from another's). The words express something irrational and dysfunctional in their erosion of cliches, slips of tongue, and confusion of codes. A type of concrete poetry, the carefully laid out text and dots establish a rhythmic flow, forming patterns of sense and nonsense. Spoonerisms, such as "chints charming", "butterpillars caterflys", "as the flow cries", "paddle tennis taddle pennis paddle taddle tennis", "it's a meal mystery", give voice to the pleasures of language play. Derived from research studies on slips of speech, they express the power of enunciation.

Metaphorically working through babble to speech, Lackey searches out and records intuitive patterns that reaffirm individuality. In her works, various notational systems are presented as programmes or hypertexts, whose links and networks are mediums of thought that rely on juxtaposition and simultaneity. Lackey engages language systems that are both software and hardware, message and medium and, thus, avoids the literal metaphors of mimesis. Lackey's interpretation of the matrix of body and language is anchored in a feminist understanding of the technologized body. In not representing the human figure as such, she effectively troubles representations of the body through conceptual means. Like many contemporary artists, she is interested in recasting the electronic realm in human and sensory terms, an impulse that has been called 'corpo-electronics.' [10] Lackey's maps of interior geographies reflect a sensibility similar to artists, such as Ann Hamilton and Mona Hatoum, who also take a rigourous, poetic approach to this subject.

odonata

1996

double-sided photo etchings

ink on paper, aluminum/plexiglas hinged frame

10 x 22.5 x 1 to 11in (25 x 56 x 2 to 28cm)

More specifically, her work engages feminist discourses that articulate knowledge through the body, an issue that has become increasingly complex with virtual realities. Lackey realizes these inquiries through traditional mediums and methods in a way that maintains the immediacy of both the senses and the digital.

Together, Lackey's works reveal a disposition that is respectful of the impulse to order experience. Any accidents, anomalies, or deviations from pattern, while only temporary aberrations, are essential assertions of an idiosyncratic individual-of life. The necessity of chance and the contingent is articulated by Foucault: "At the most basic level of life, the processes of coding and decoding give way to a chance occurrence that, before becoming a disease, a deficiency, or a monstrosity, is something like a disturbance in the informative system, something like a 'mistake.' In this sense, life – and this is its radical feature – is that which is capable of error. And perhaps it is this datum or rather this contingency which must be asked to account for the fact that the question of anomaly permeates the whole of biology." [11]

Without throwing away archiving systems of classification and taxonomy, Lackey works within measured frameworks to give voice to these contingencies. Measurement is at the core of her project, evident in her preoccupation with binary relationships. Questions of classification, likeness, and category arise from the paired images of *'magnifications: cell (2); cell (1)'*, *'receptors: scrape/swab'*, and *'new centuries: vol. 1 and 2'* . Lackey's binary aesthetic reiterates the rhetoric of analogy. In forcing comparisons, these pieces provoke a search for linkages and pattern, creating an awareness of the mutability of the dualities of brain/body, text/image, inside/outside. The busy networks of equivalences that permeate Lackey's pieces ask to be tallied, sorted, differentiated, and categorized yet, in this process, we realize there are infinite combinations and permutations: nothing is fixed.

smear (3)
1999
acrylic, ink on cork, birch plywood
44.5 x 45 x 4in (111 x 112 x 10cm)

Lackey's notational systems invite the viewer to scan, count, decode, and make sense of visual stimuli through durational procedures that, in effect, slow down time. Scrolling vertically and horizontally through the accretions of data involves a continual process of synthesis and fusion. Lackey's contemplative works are finely calibrated spaces that slowly unravel habits of mind. In an effort to turn down the high pitched velocity of data that invades contemporary experience – to begin to integrate that information – the artist responds from solid ground, from an embodied knowledge. In returning technological language to material visuality and the world of the observer, she affirms the experiential richness of the technological imaginary. Her artworks express the convergences of natural and artificial life as a type of Mobius strip where perpetual mutation articulates and conceals knowledge.

Helga Pakasaar
writer and curator
Windsor, Canada

1. For example, the Jacquard loom with its punch card mechanism for lifting warp yarns helped to inspire the invention of the first computer, Charles Babbage's 'Analytical Engine' of 1843, and the algebraic patterns and grids of layered electronic information contained in microchips function much like a loom.

2. The inscrutability of nature that defined traditional notions of the sublime could now be said to be a property of technology. The influence of electronic media on the contemporary sublime has been discussed in texts by Jeremy Gilbert-Rolfe, *Beauty and the Contemporary Sublime* (New York: Allworth Press, 1999), and Marek Wieczorek, *The SmArt Gene (or, Are We Not Alone in Our Esthetic Universe?)* (Seattle, Washington: Henry Art Gallery (gene)sis Web site 2002), who also considers the sublime in relation to the genome.

3. Jane Lackey, notes for the exhibition 'in code,' Grand Arts, Kansas City, Missouri, 1996.

4. Ibid.

5. Michel Foucault, *The Order of Things* (New York: Vintage Books, 1973), p. 34.

6. Hattie Gordon, 'Feast,' in *Anne Wilson*, (Portfolio Collection vol. 6, Winchester, England: Telos Art Publishing, 2001), p. 45.

7. The fact that bees are now being trained by Pentagon-funded research to sniff out explosives is indicative of how scientific knowledge acquires complex social ramifications, as do all the languages in Lackey's works.

8. Naomi Schor, in *Reading in Detail: Aesthetics and the Feminine* (New York and London: Methuen, 1987), proposes a feminist reading of the social significance of detail, ornament and the decorative.

9. Jane Lackey, unpublished notes, 2001.

10. See Christine Ross, 'To Touch the Other,' in *Touch in Contemporary Art* (Toronto, Ontario: Public Access, 1996), pp. 48-61.

11. Michel Foucault, 'Life: Experience and Science,' *Aesthetics, Method, and Epistemology* (New York: The New Press, 1998), p. 476.

opposite:
webster's line
1999
Installation, Cranbrook Art Museum
dictionaries, polyurethane
9.5 x 180 x 1.75in (24 x 450 x 4cm)

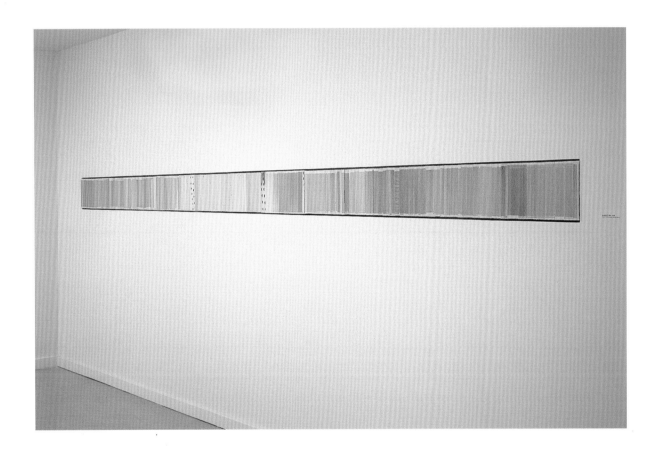

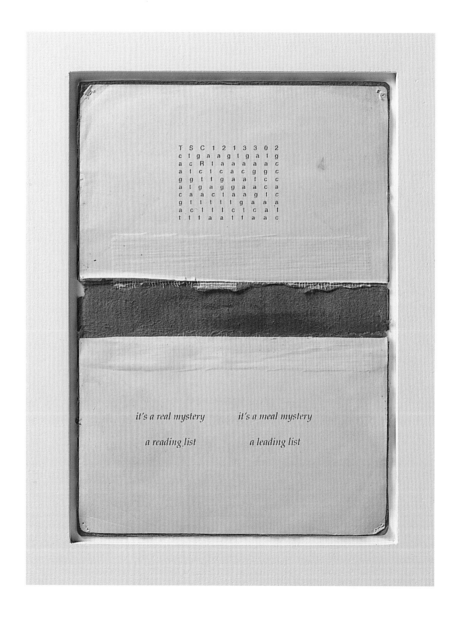

SNPS/slips

SNPS/slips 1

2002
dictionary, laser engraving,
lacquer/wood frame
20 x 24 x 2.75in
(50 x 60 x 7cm)

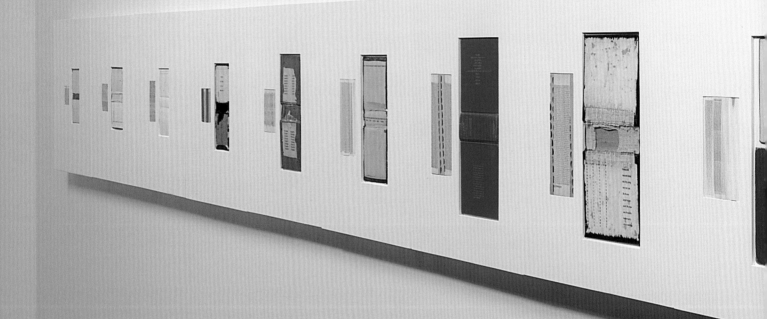

SNPS/slips

Installation of 12

2002

dictionaries, laser engraving,

lacquer/wood frames

20 x 288 x 2.75in (50 x 720 x 7cm)

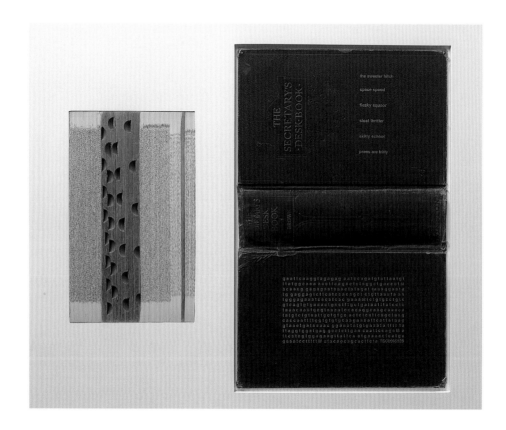

SNPS/slips 10

2002

dictionary, laser engraving,

lacquer/wood frame

20 x 24 x 2.75in (50 x 60 x 7cm)

SNPS/slips no. 9
2002
dictionaries, laser printing,
lacquer/wood frame
20 x 24 x 2.75in (50 x 60 x 7cm)

the pastor placed his hand,
the pastor paced...diner at eight, inner
at date,
Ed and Bessy, bed and essy
a whole blox of flowers, chrysanthe-
mum plants, chrysanthemun pants, if
it's any consolation...any consultation

SNPS/slips 9 (detail)
2002
dictionaries, laser engraving,
lacquer/wood frame
20 x 24 x 2.75in (50 x 60 x 7cm)

SNPS/slips 10 (detail)
2002
dictionaries, laser engravings,
lacquer/wood frame
20 x 24 x 2.75in (50 x 60 x 7cm)

Other titles in this series

Vol 6: Anne Wilson
By Tim Porges and Hattie Gordon
ISBN 1 902015 22 3 (softback)

Vol 8 :Helen Lancaster
ISBN 1 902015 29 0 (softback)
ISBN 1 902015 45 2 (hardback)

Vol 9: Kay Lawrence
ISBN 1 902015 28 2 (softback)
ISBN 1 902015 44 4 (hardback)

Vol 10: Joan Livingstone
ISBN 1 902015 27 4 (softback)
ISBN 1 902015 43 6 (hardback)

Vol 11: Marian Smit
ISBN 1 902015 32 0 (softback)
ISBN 1 902015 46 0 (hardback)

Vol 12: Tanaka Chiyoko
ISBN 1 902015 24 X (softback)
ISBN 1 902015 42 8 (hardback)

Vol 14: Lia Cook (Sept 02)
ISBN 1 902015 34 7 (softback)
ISBN 1 902015 51 7 (hardback)

Vol 15: Jane Lackey (Sept 02)
ISBN 1 902015 35 5 (softback)
ISBN 1 902015 52 5 (hardback)

Vol 16: Gerhardt Knodel (Sept 02)
ISBN 1 902015 47 9 (softback)
ISBN 1 902015 48 7 (hardback)

Vol 17:Kyoung Ae Cho (Feb 03)
ISBN 1 902015 35 5 (softback)
ISBN 1 902015 50 9 (hardback)

Vol 18: Jason Pollen (Feb 03)
ISBN 1 902015 74 6 (softback)
ISBN (hardback)

Vol 19: Barbara Layne (Feb 03)
ISBN 1 902015 36 3 (softback)
ISBN 1 902015 76 2 (hardback)

Vol 20: Kay Sekimachi (Feb 03)
ISBN 1 902015 77 0 (softback)
ISBN 1 902015 78 9 (hardback)

Vol 21: Emily DuBois (Feb 03)
ISBN 1 902015 38 X (softback)
ISBN 1 902015 54 1 (hardback)

Vol 22: Gyongy Laky (Feb 03)
ISBN 1 902015 39 8 (softback)
ISBN 1 902015 56 8 (hardback)

Vol 23: Virginia Davis (Feb 03)
ISBN 1 902015 40 1 (softback)
ISBN 1 902015 57 6 (hardback)

Vol 24: Piper Shepard (Feb 03)
ISBN 1 902015 81 9 (softback)
ISBN 1 902015 82 7 (hardback)

Vol 25: Valerie Kirk (Feb 03)
ISBN 1 902015 37 1 (softback)
ISBN 1 902015 55 X (hardback)

Vol 26: Annet Couwenberg (Feb 03)
ISBN 1 902015 79 7 (softback)
ISBN 1 902015 80 0 (hardback)

Vol 27: Susan Lordi Marker (Feb 03)
ISBN 1 902015 41 X (softback)
ISBN 1 902015 58 4 (hardback)

Vol 28: Agano Machiko (Feb 03)
ISBN 1 902015 59 2 (softback)
ISBN 1 902015 60 6 (hardback)

Vol 29: Fukumoto Shihoko (Feb 03)
ISBN 1 902015 61 4 (softback)
ISBN 1 902015622 (hardback)

Vol 30: Cynthia Schira (Feb 03)
ISBN 1 902015 63 0 (softback)
ISBN 1 902015 64 9 (hardback)

Vol 31: Kumai Kyoko (Sept 03)
ISBN 1 902015 65 7 (softback)
ISBN 1 902015 66 5 (hardback)

Vol 32: Suzie Brandt (Sept 03)
ISBN 1 902015 67 3 (softback)
ISBN 1 902015 68 1 (hardback)

Vol 33: Darrel Morris (Sept 03)
ISBN 1 902015 69 X (softback)
ISBN 1 902015 70 3 (hardback)

Vol 34: Pauline Burbidge (Feb 04)
ISBN 1 902015 71 1 (softback)
ISBN 1 902015 72 X (hardback)

Visit www.telos.net for further details